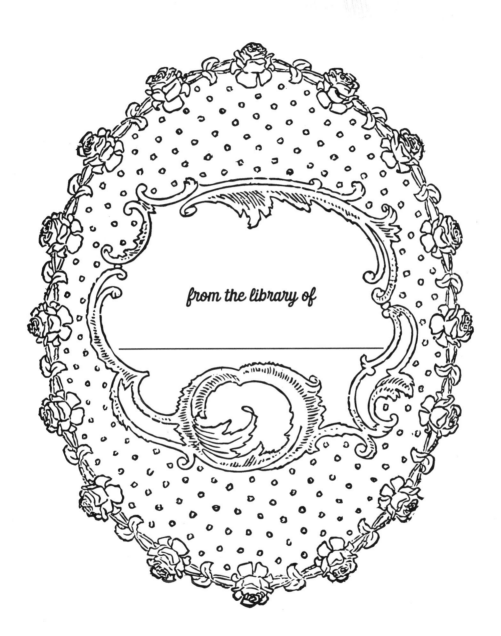

from the library of

_____

girls will be boys
will be girls will be ...

Jacinta Bunnell

More coloring books from PM Press and Reach and Teach

Girls Are Not Chicks
Jacinta Bunnell & Julie Novak

Sometimes the Spoon Runs Away with Another Spoon
Jacinta Bunnell & Nathaniel Kusinitz

The Big Gay Alphabet
Jacinta Bunnell & Leela Corman

Girls Will Be Boys Will Be Girls Will Be ... Coloring Book
Jacinta Bunnell

ISBN: 978-1-62963-507-1

Copyright © 2018 Jacinta Bunnell
This edition copyright © 2018 PM Press
All Rights Reserved

Cover design: Giselle Potter, Jacinta Bunnell, Jonathan Rowland, and Michael Wilcock
Cover illustration by Giselle Potter, colored by Jacinta Bunnell and Michael Wilcock
Layout & Design: Jacinta Bunnell, Michael Wilcock, and Jonathan Rowland
Daily Grind font © BLKBK www.blkbktyp.com

www.queerbookcommittee.com

PM Press
PO Box 23912
Oakland, CA 94623
www.pmpress.org

Reach And Teach
144 W. 25th Avenue
San Mateo, CA 94403
www.reachandteach.com

Printed in the USA

When gender is a binary, it's a battlefield. When you get
rid of the binary, gender becomes a playground.
–Kate Bornstein

You are amazing grace.
You are a precious jewel.
You–special, miraculous, unrepeatable, fragile, fearful, tender,
lost, sparkling ruby emerald jewel, rainbow splendor person.
–Joan Baez

The soul that lives inside this body will
not be ignored. I am here to stay.
–RuPaul

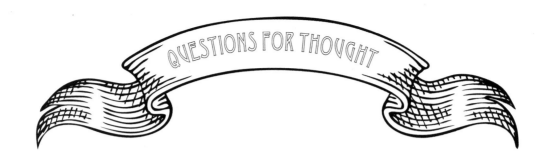

How do you define gender?

In what ways is gender a spectrum?

What would the world look like without a gender binary?

How has the proliferation of a gender binary impacted you?

In what ways do you feel confined or restricted by your assigned gender?

Was the gender assigned to you the one you feel most comfortable with?

In what ways do you play with gender?

What privileges do you or don't you have due to the gender you have been labeled?

What is your gender story?

What do you love about gender?

Are there ways in which your gender identity has been silenced or judged?

In what ways do you resist or embrace gender fluidity?

How do you celebrate gender in your life?

What is the future of gender?

Don't let gender box you in.

Illustration by Quinn Russell

Toys have no gender.

Illustration by Quinn Russell

We'll decide for ourselves what girls can be.

Illustration by Kristine Virsis

Girls Will Be Boys Will Be Girls Will Be... by Jacinta Bunnell

There's more to being boys than what they told us.

Illustration by Lex Lethal

Enough about our forefathers, let's learn about
some revolutionary drag kings and queens!

Illustration by Julie Novak

This life is filled with heroic handsome beauties.

Illustration by Nicole Rodrigues

Boys on strike.

Illustration by Michael Wilcock

Babies against gender assignment.

Illustration by Hopie Windle

How's this for ladylike?!

Illustration by Jacinta Bunnell

Sometimes the princess is saved by the friend next door.

Illustration by Elokin Orton-Cheung

I should have worn a skirt.
The pants bathroom is all full.

Illustration by Quinn Russell

See what I mean? You wouldn't like it either!

I'm not about that, mom!

Illustration by Jacinta Bunnell

At the age of five, I decided to stop serving him.

Illustration by Nicole Georges

Hug Club.

Illustration by Mark Swier

Grandpa, when we finish knitting, can we bake quiche together?

Illustration by Michael Wilcock

Cole likes to nurture...

Illustration by Shane Ballard

...and be nurtured.

Illustration by Shane Ballard

I guess Mom really meant it when she said she wasn't doing the dishes anymore.

Illustration by Michael Asbill

What's in your gender recipe?

Illustration by Richard Wentworth

Keetin is getting ready to teach the neighborhood how to fix a flat.

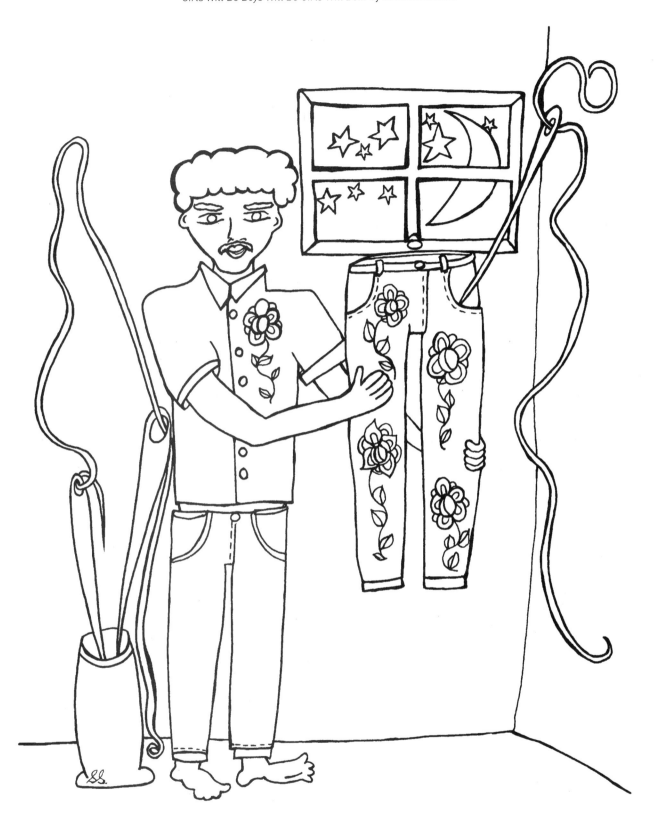

Stanley sews slacks on Super Bowl Sunday.

Illustration by Simi Stone

Me and my boy Tommy got 98% on our Man Tests.
What did you get?

Illustration by Paul Heath

The future is gender fabulous.

Illustration by Laura Ann Newburn

Dad, after we're done tidying the living room, let's go clean up toxic masculinity together.

Illustration by Amanda Fucello

Aunt Wanda really knows machines.

Illustration by Michael Wilcock

Rise up. The future is ours. Together we shall prevail.

Illustration by Giselle Potter

Gender Menu

GENDERQUEER	TRANS	BURRNESHA	GENDER DIVERSE	GENDER CREATIVE
TRANSGENDER	DRAG KING	NONBINARY TRANS	BOY	MAHU
GENDER EXPANSIVE	TWO-SPIRIT	TRANSFEMININE	KATHOEY	BUTCH QUEEN
NEITHER-GENDER	AGENDER	KHANITH	ANDROGYNOUS	WOMAN
BUTCH	BOI	INTERSEX	BANJEE	GENDER QUESTIONING
GENDER BENDER	YAN DAUDU	GIRL	GIRL-BOY	FEMININE PRESENTING
FAKALEITI	TRANSMASCULINE	MUXE	TWINK	CIS WOMAN
QUESTIONING	PANGENDER	TRANS MAN	NEUTROIS	DEMIBOY
GENDER NON-CONFORMING	FA'AFAFINE	GENDER VARIANT	FEMME QUEEN	NONBINARY
CIS	GENDERLESS	TRIGENDER	MAN	CISGENDER
MASCULINE PRESENTING	HIJRA	BULL DYKE	TOMBOY	QUEEN
TRANS WOMAN	POLYGENDER	BOY-GIRL	BIGENDER	FEMME
INTERGENDER	DRAG QUEEN	DEMIGIRL	CIS MAN	FLUID
TRANSCENDING GENDER	GENDER CURIOUS	GENDER FABULOUS	GENDERFLUID	ANDROGYNE

Thank goodness there's no more prix fixe menu!

Illustration by Michael Wilcock

You are the gender of your wildest dreams.

Illustration by Jac Dellaria

ACKNOWLEDGMENTS

I owe colossal gratitude to Irit Reinheimer, my lifetime confidant and co-conspirator, who sat with me on futons, unyielding computer lab chairs, and college library floors scheming up a zine that would one day be this book. The year was 2001, and all we had to help us with distribution was the email address colormegenderless@facehugger.com and a post office box.

My work and friendship with Irit has forever shaped who I am and has led to over a decade of publishing coloring books about gender creativity and feminism, which is the dream job I never knew existed. Without Irit, I would not be so contented, nor would this book exist.

This book has seen many incarnations. It's been self-published, living in boxes taking up half of my living room. It's seen one publisher go out of business. May it now find peace in its new home with PM Press and Reach & Teach, who have taken a chance on me and my ideas for so many years. It is they who gently nudged me to bring this book back to life. I am grateful to them for believing in me.

Thank you to Michael Asbill, Shane Ballard, Jac Dellaria, Amanda Fucello, Nicole Georges, Paul Heath, Lex Lethal, Laura Ann Newburn, Julie Novak, Elokin Orton-Cheung, Giselle Potter, Nicole Rodrigues, Quinn Russell, Simi Stone, Mark Swier, Kristine Virsis, Rich Wentworth, Michael Wilcock, and Hopie Windle, who all contributed their fabulous art to this book. When we get together, there isn't anything we can't be ... and I believe this is a terrific place to start.

I believe you.

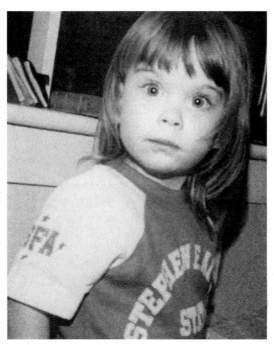

Jacinta Bunnell is the author of three other coloring books: *Sometimes the Spoon Runs Away with Another Spoon*, *Girls Are Not Chicks*, and *The Big Gay Alphabet*. Jacinta was once banned by her family from going out to dinner at Gentleman Jim's Steakhouse because she refused to wear a dress. But she went on to co-found a costumed philanthropic ladies' arm wrestling league, so who's laughing now?

ABOUT REACH AND TEACH

Reach And Teach is a peace and social justice learning company, transforming the world through teachable moments. They publish and distribute books, music, posters, games, curriculum, and DVDs that focus on peacemaking and healing the planet.

Reach And Teach
144 W. 25th Ave.
San Mateo, CA 94403
www.reachandteach.com

ABOUT PM PRESS

PM Press was founded at the end of 2007 by a small collection of folks with decades of publishing, media, and organizing experience. PM Press co-conspirators have published and distributed hundreds of books, pamphlets, CDs, and DVDs. Members of PM have founded enduring book fairs, spearheaded victorious tenant organizing campaigns, and worked closely with bookstores, academic conferences, and even rock bands to deliver political and challenging ideas to all walks of life. We're old enough to know what we're doing and young enough to know what's at stake.

We seek to create radical and stimulating fiction and nonfiction books, pamphlets, T-shirts, visual and audio materials to entertain, educate, and inspire you. We aim to distribute these through every available channel with every available technology, whether that means you are seeing anarchist classics at our bookfair stalls; reading our latest vegan cookbook at the café; downloading geeky fiction e-books; or digging new music and timely videos from our website.

Contact us for direct ordering and questions about all PM Press releases, as well as manuscript submissions, review copy requests, foreign rights sales, author interviews, to book an author for an event, and to have PM Press attend your bookfair:

PM Press
PO Box 23912
Oakland, CA 94623
Buy books and stay on top of what we are doing at: www.pmpress.org

FRIENDS OF PM PRESS MONTHLY SUBSCRIPTION PROGRAM

In the many years since its founding—and on a mere shoestring—PM Press has risen to the formidable challenge of publishing and distributing knowledge and entertainment for the struggles ahead. With hundreds of releases to date, we have published an impressive and stimulating array of literature, art, music, politics, and culture. Using every available medium, we've succeeded in connecting those hungry for ideas and information to those putting them into practice.

Friends of PM allows you to directly help impact, amplify, and revitalize the discourse and actions of radical writers, filmmakers, and artists. It provides us with a stable foundation from which we can build upon our early successes and provides a much-needed subsidy for the materials that can't necessarily pay their own way. You can help make that happen—and receive every new title automatically delivered to your door once a month—by joining as a Friend of PM Press. And, we'll throw in a free T-shirt when you sign up.

Here are your options:

- **$30 a month: Get all books and pamphlets plus 50% discount on all webstore purchases**
- **$40 a month**: Get all PM Press releases (including CDs and DVDs) plus 50% discount on all webstore purchases
- **$100 a month**: Superstar—Everything above plus PM merchandise and free downloads

For those who can't afford $30 or more a month, we're introducing **Sustainer Rates** at $15, $10, and $5. Sustainers get a free PM Press T-shirt and a 50% discount on all purchases from our website.

Your Visa or Mastercard will be billed once a month, until you tell us to stop. Or until our efforts succeed in bringing the revolution around. Or the financial meltdown of Capital makes plastic redundant. Whichever comes first.